BONUS

I0462449

Pick up your FREE BONUS sweary word coloring pages!

Check out: **www.FckYeahColoring.com**

For more BONUS pages like this...

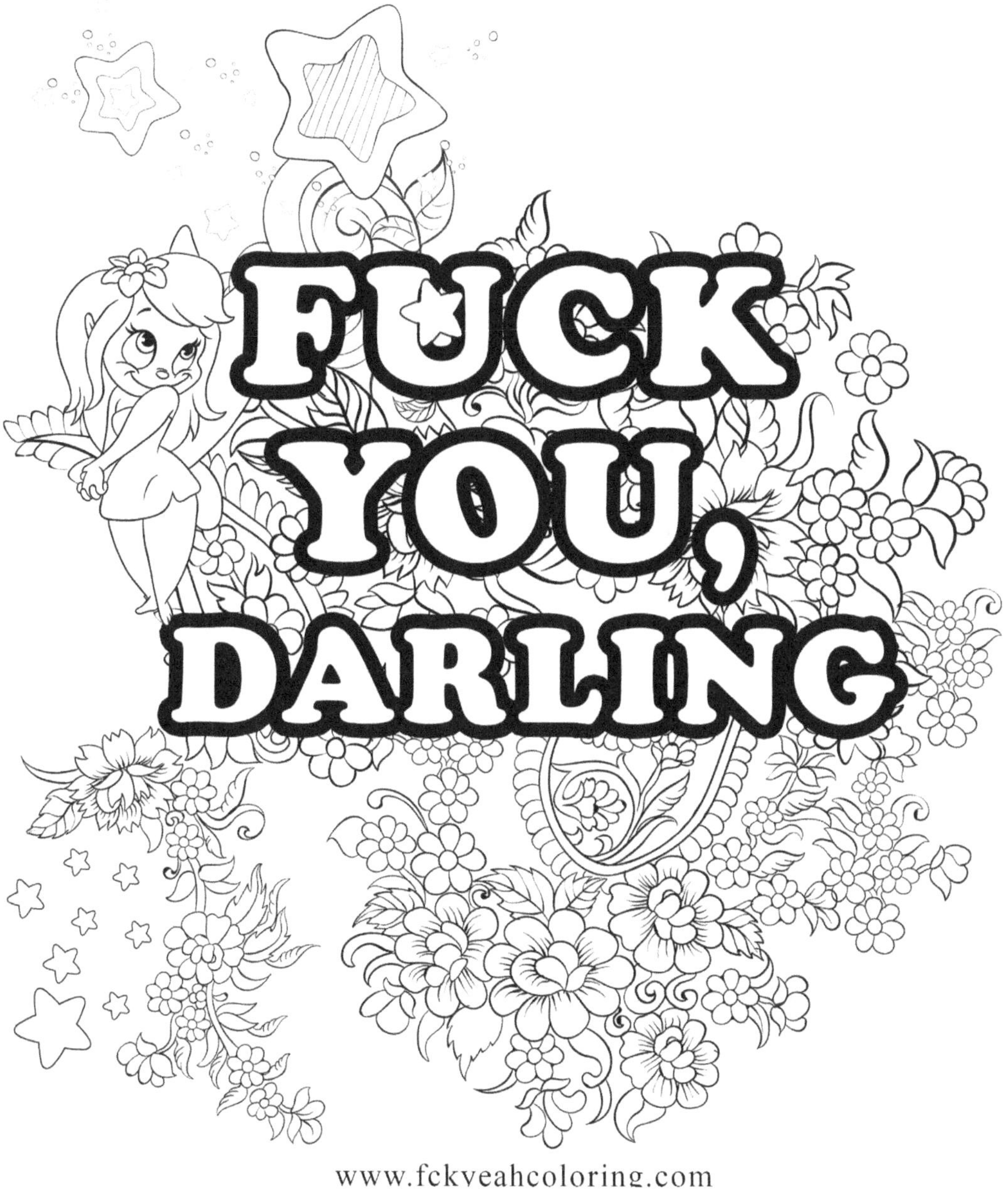

www.fckyeahcoloring.com

Dear Creative,

Have a giggle and blow off some steam!

Look through the pages, and pick out the swears that speak to you at the moment.

Just remember, these pages are 18+ and not for the faint-hearted!

I send out NEW, FREE bonus pages every couple of weeks

as a special thank you.

Grab your ridiculously crude new pages at **www.FckYeahColoring.com**

Make sure you get printable BONUS sweary coloring pages

delivered immediately!

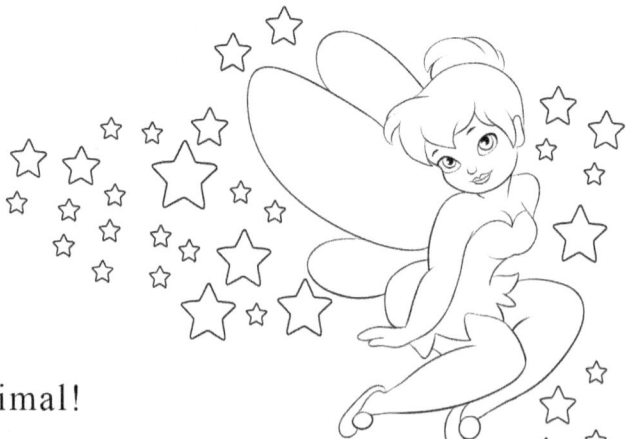

Now, enjoy coloring, you filthy animal!

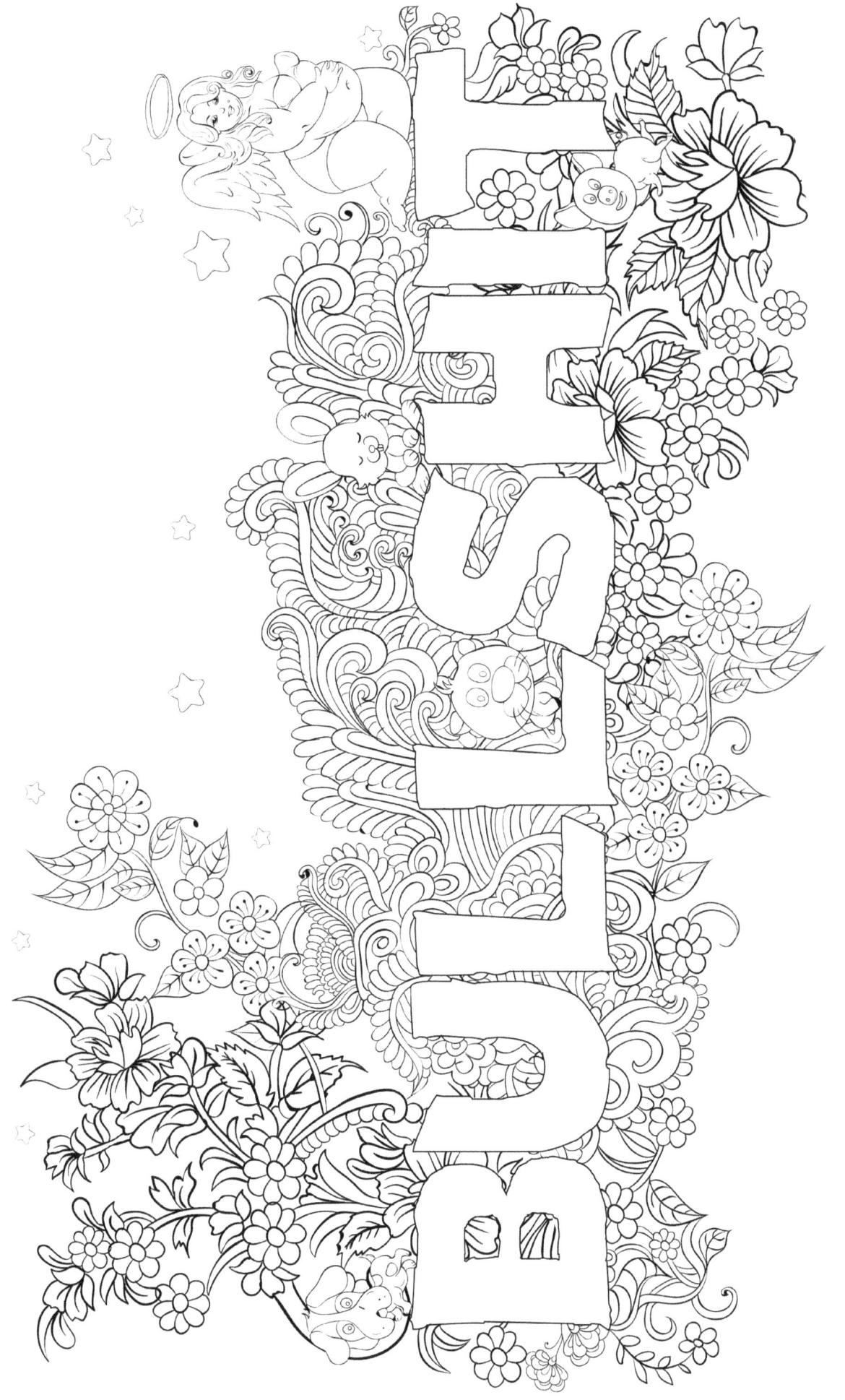

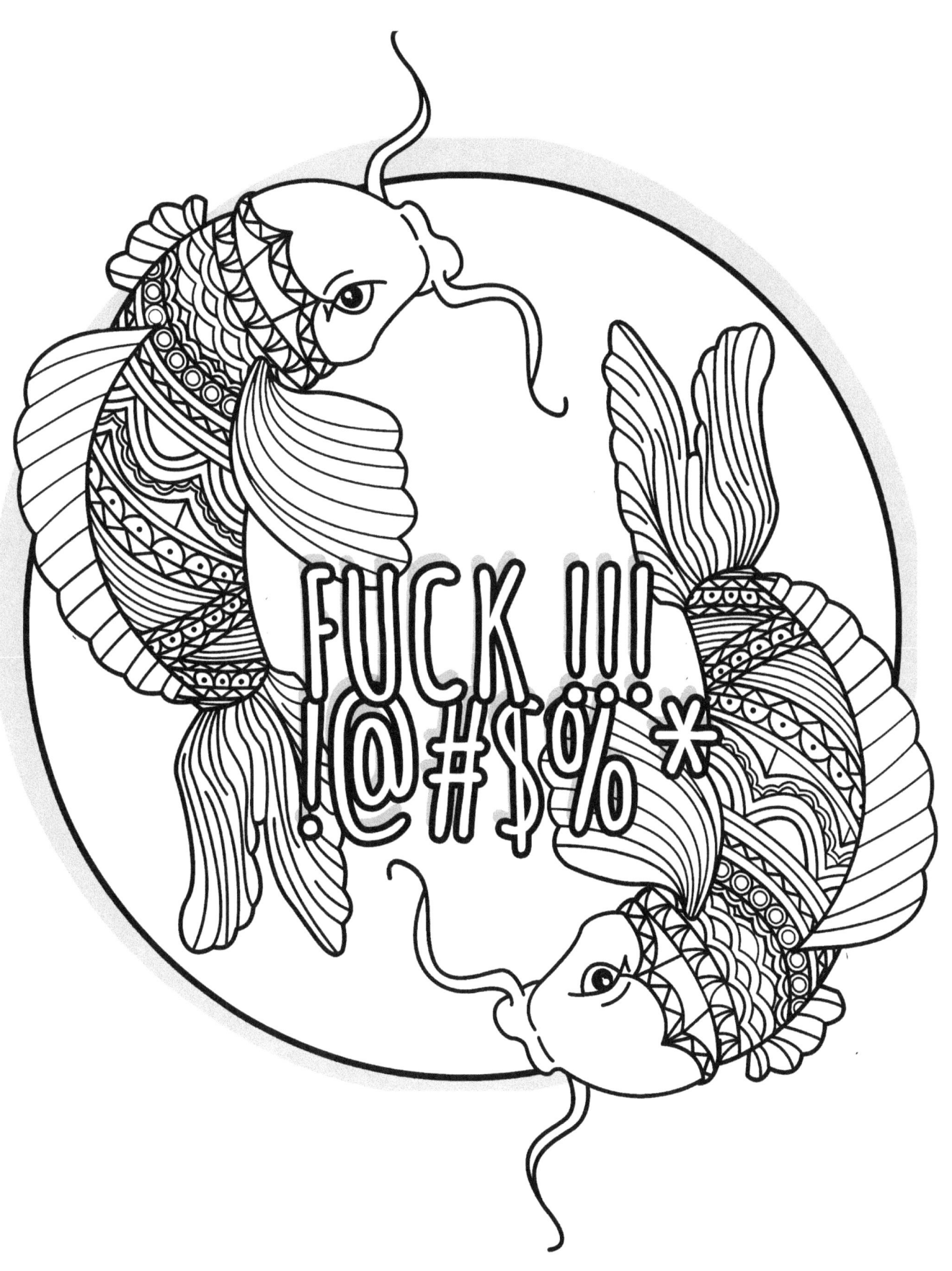

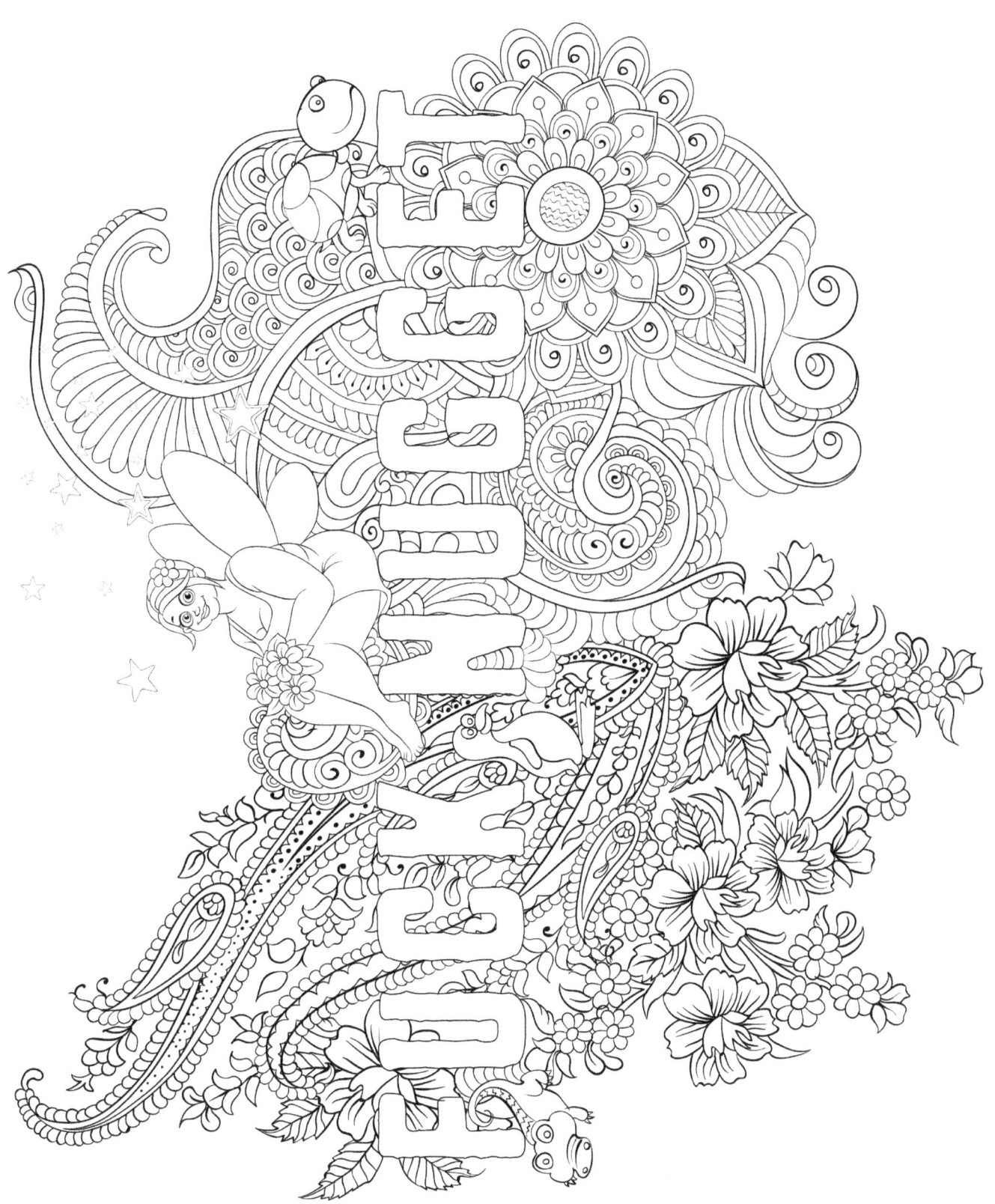

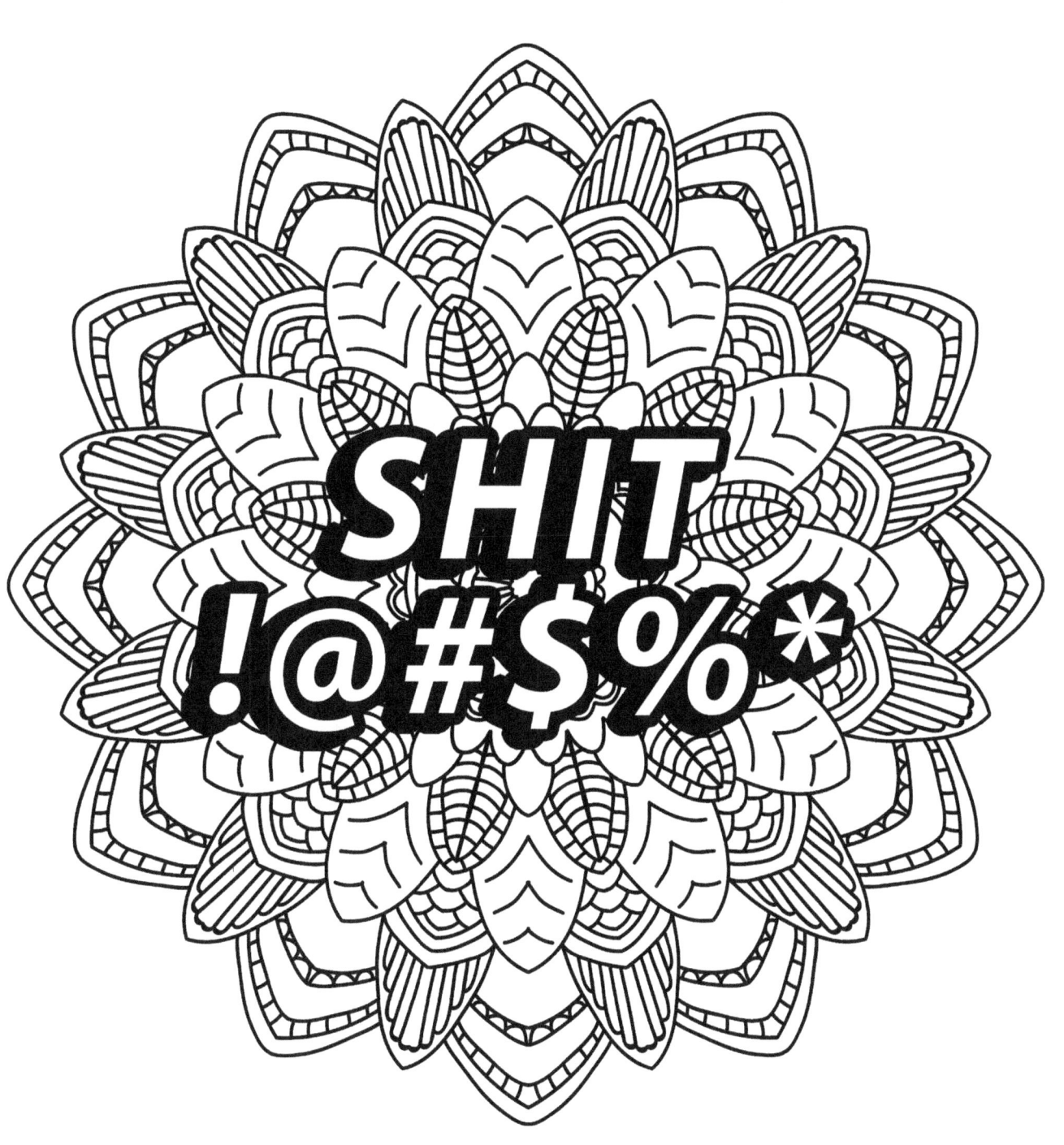

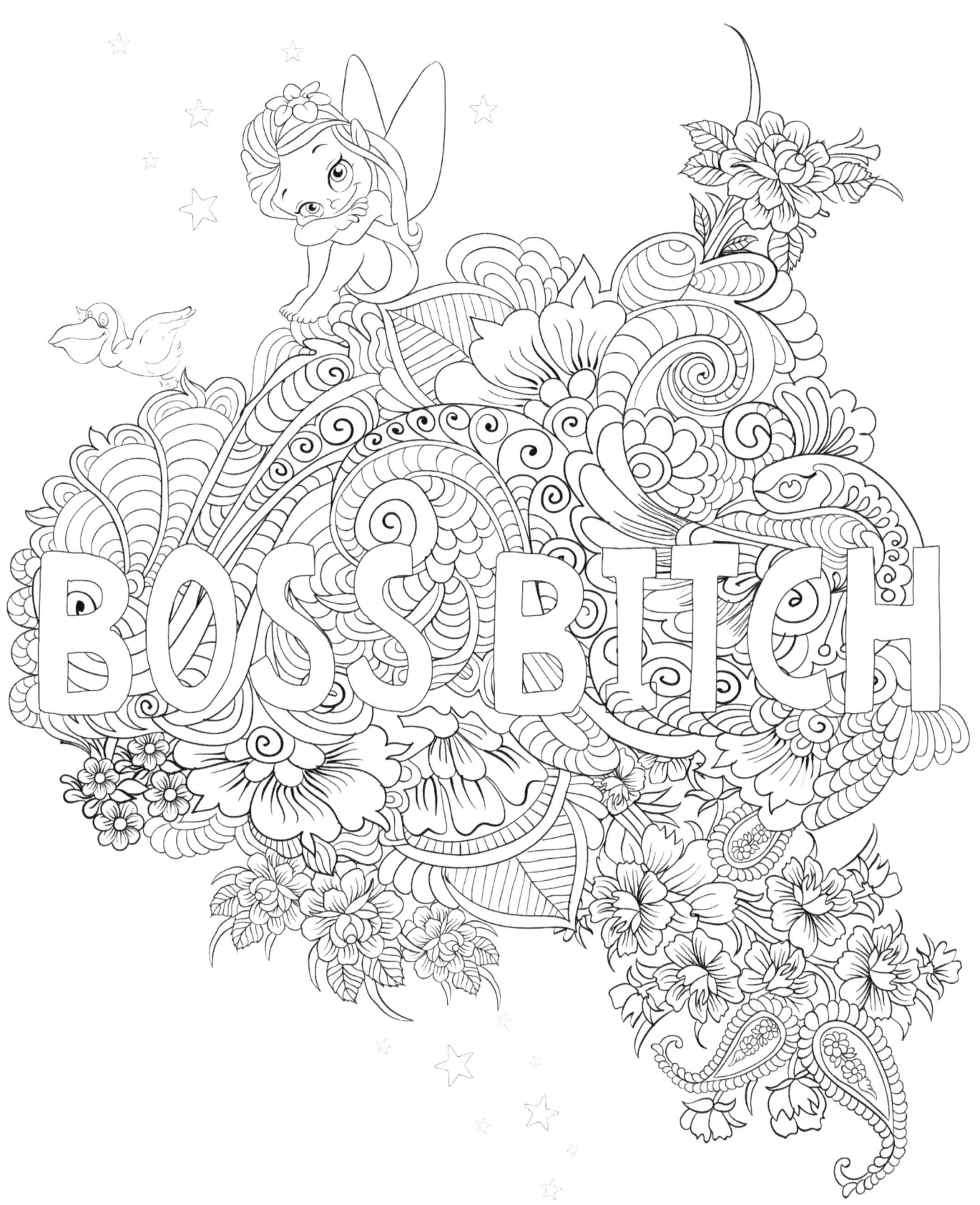

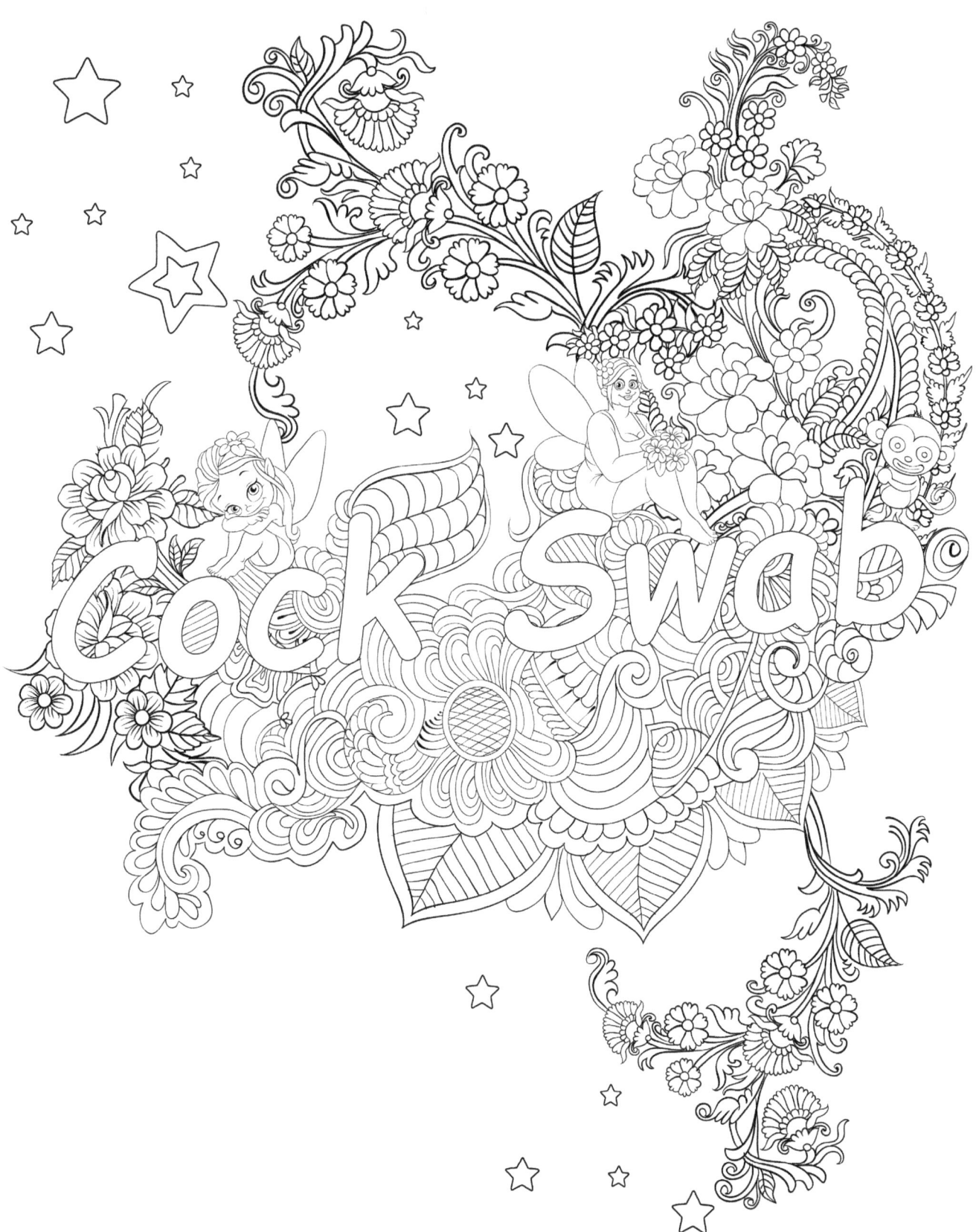

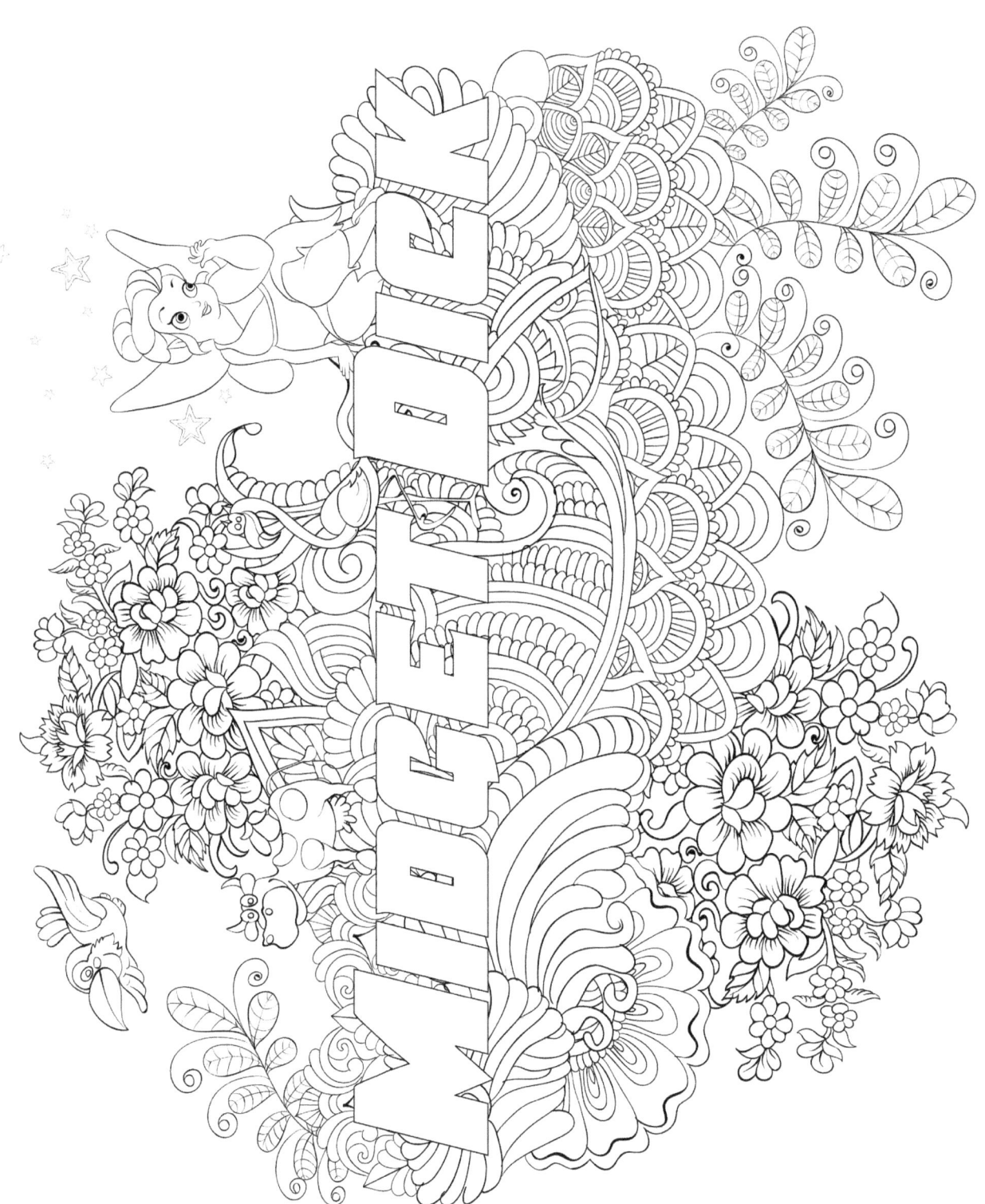

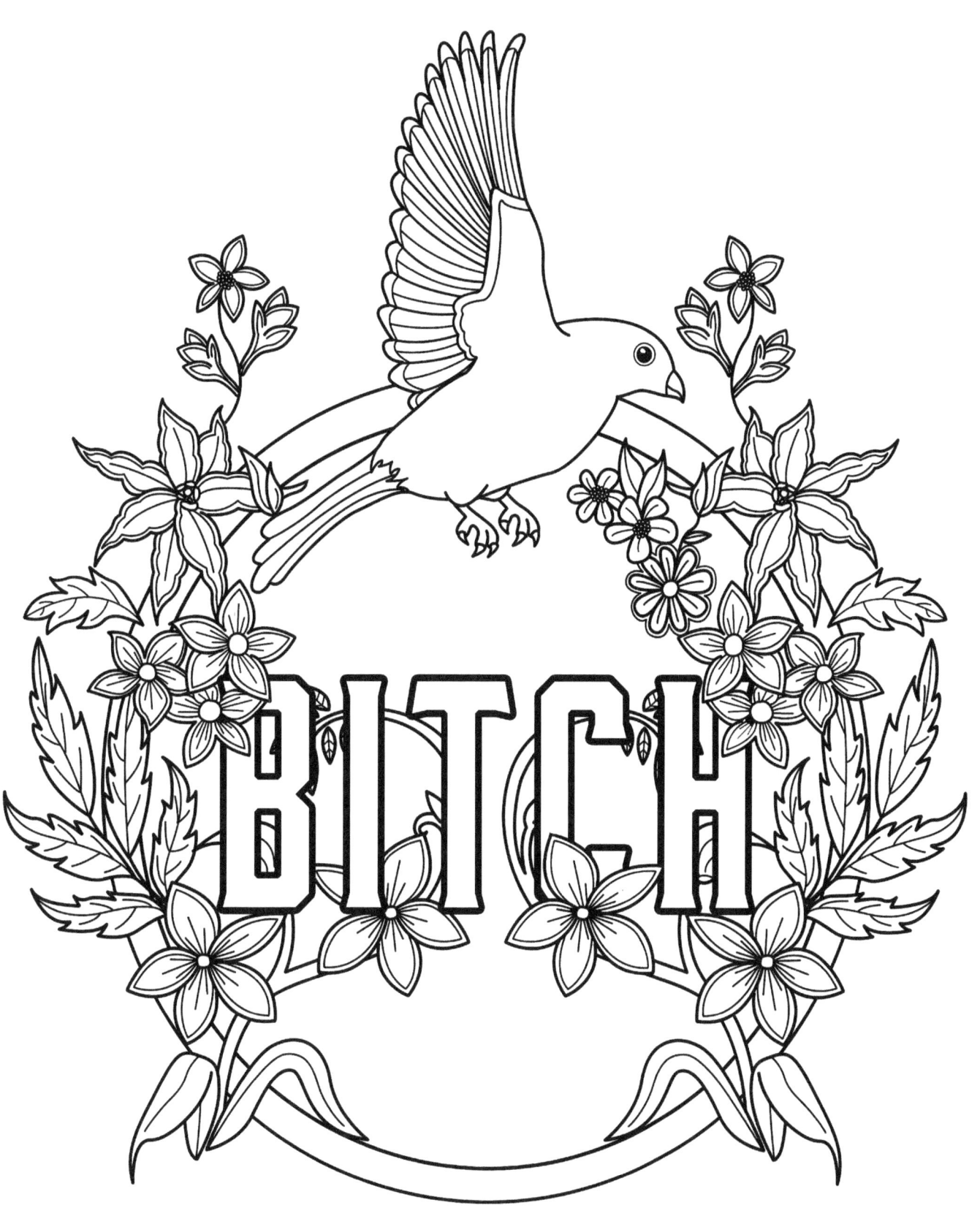

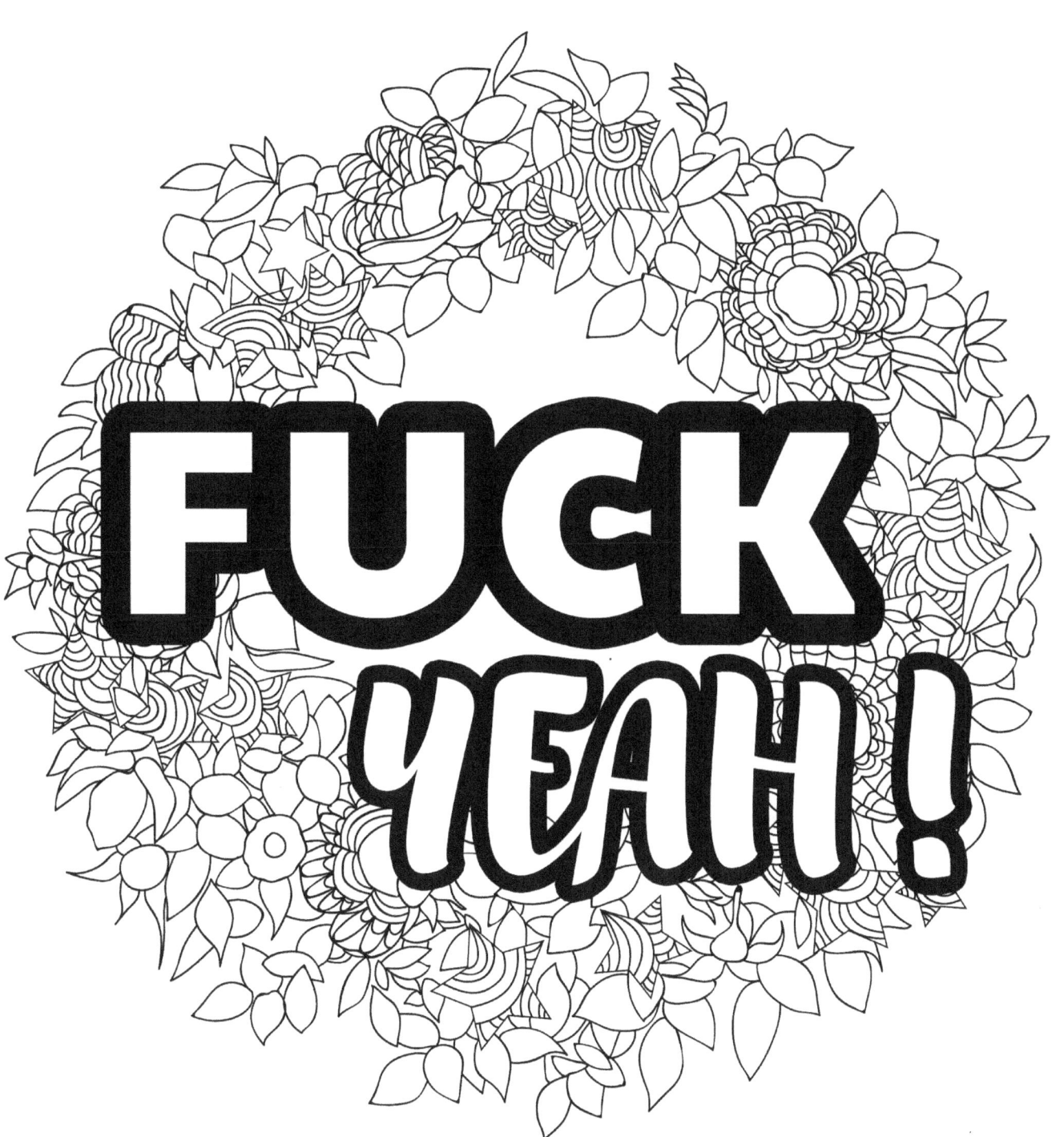

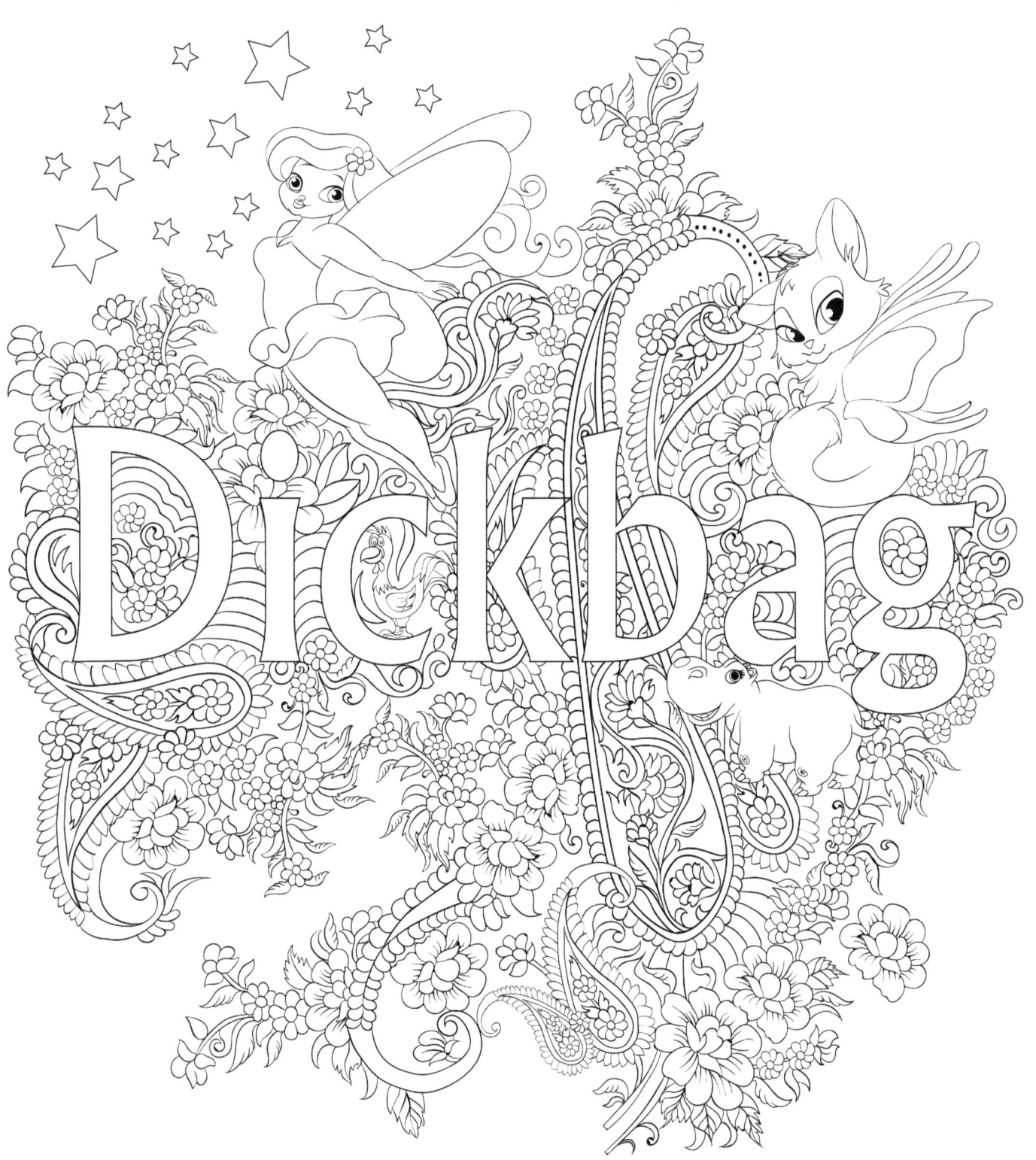

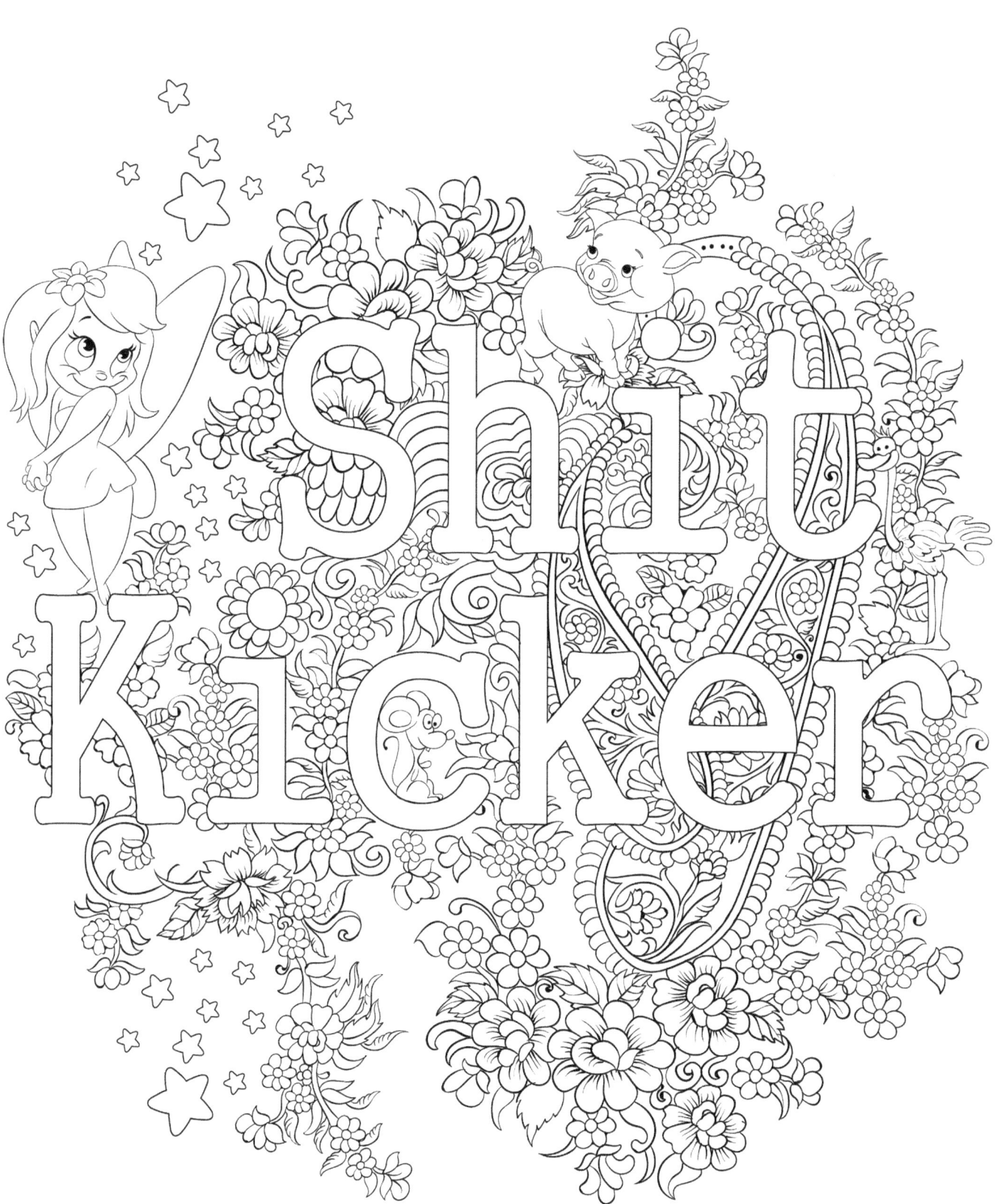

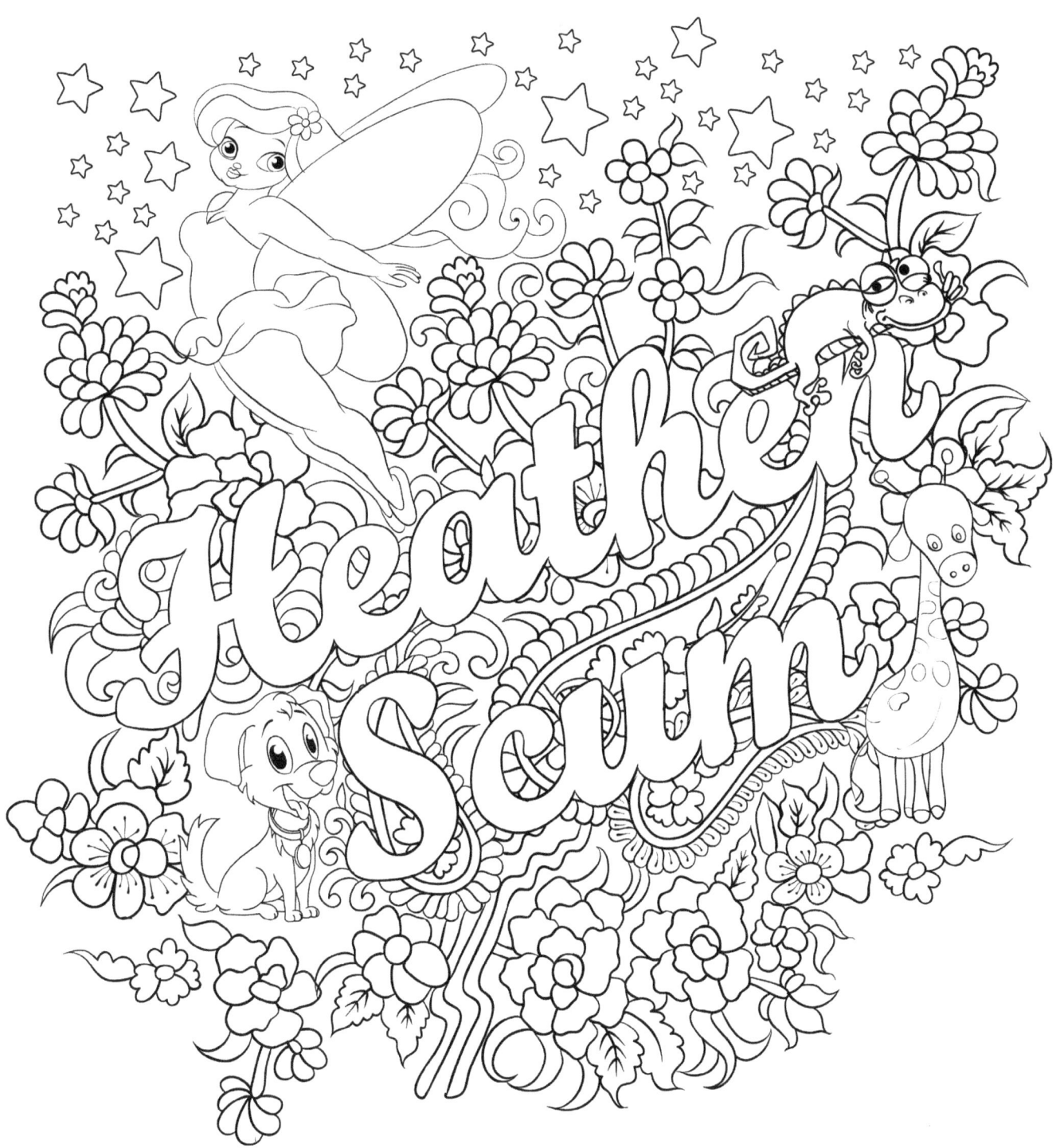

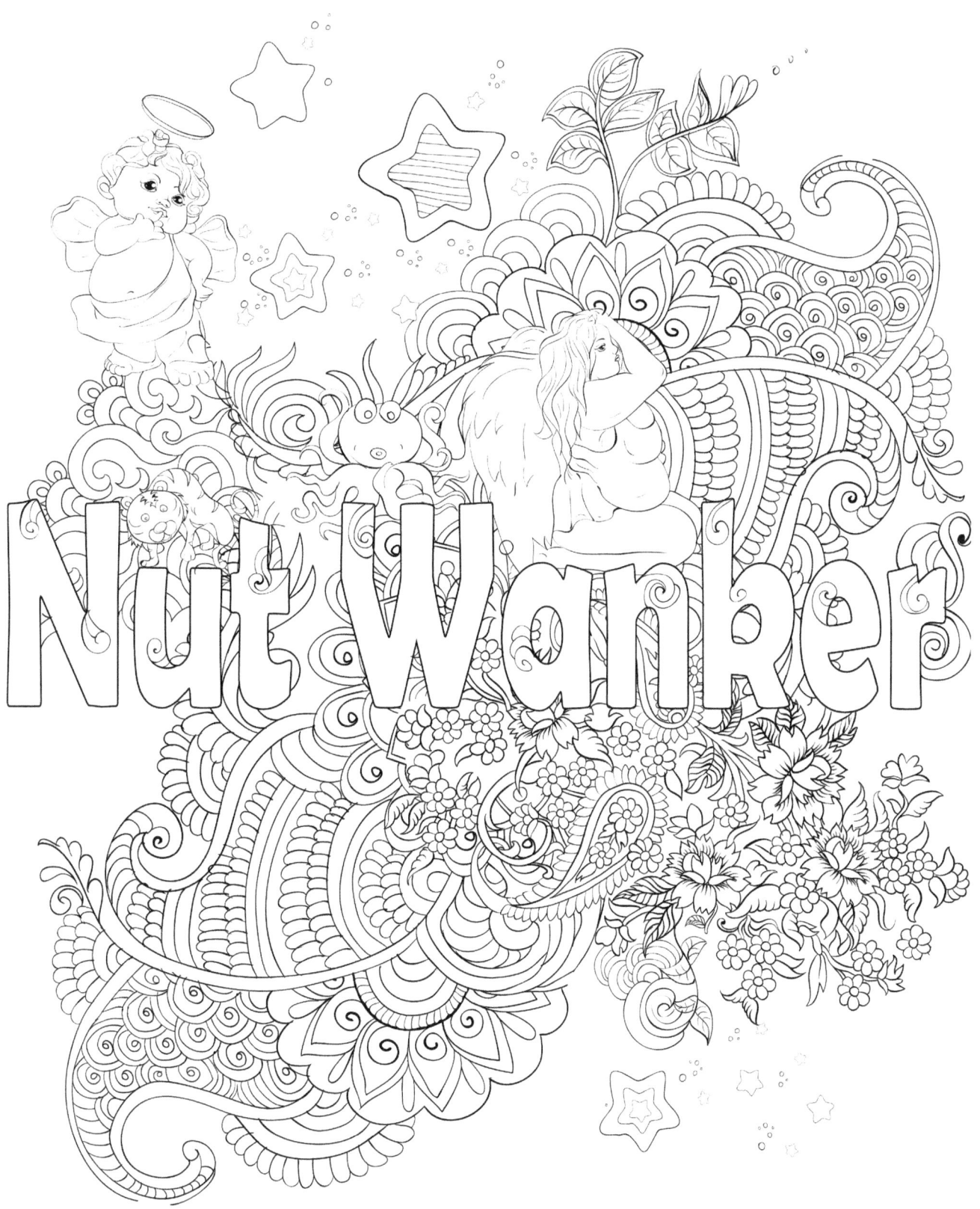

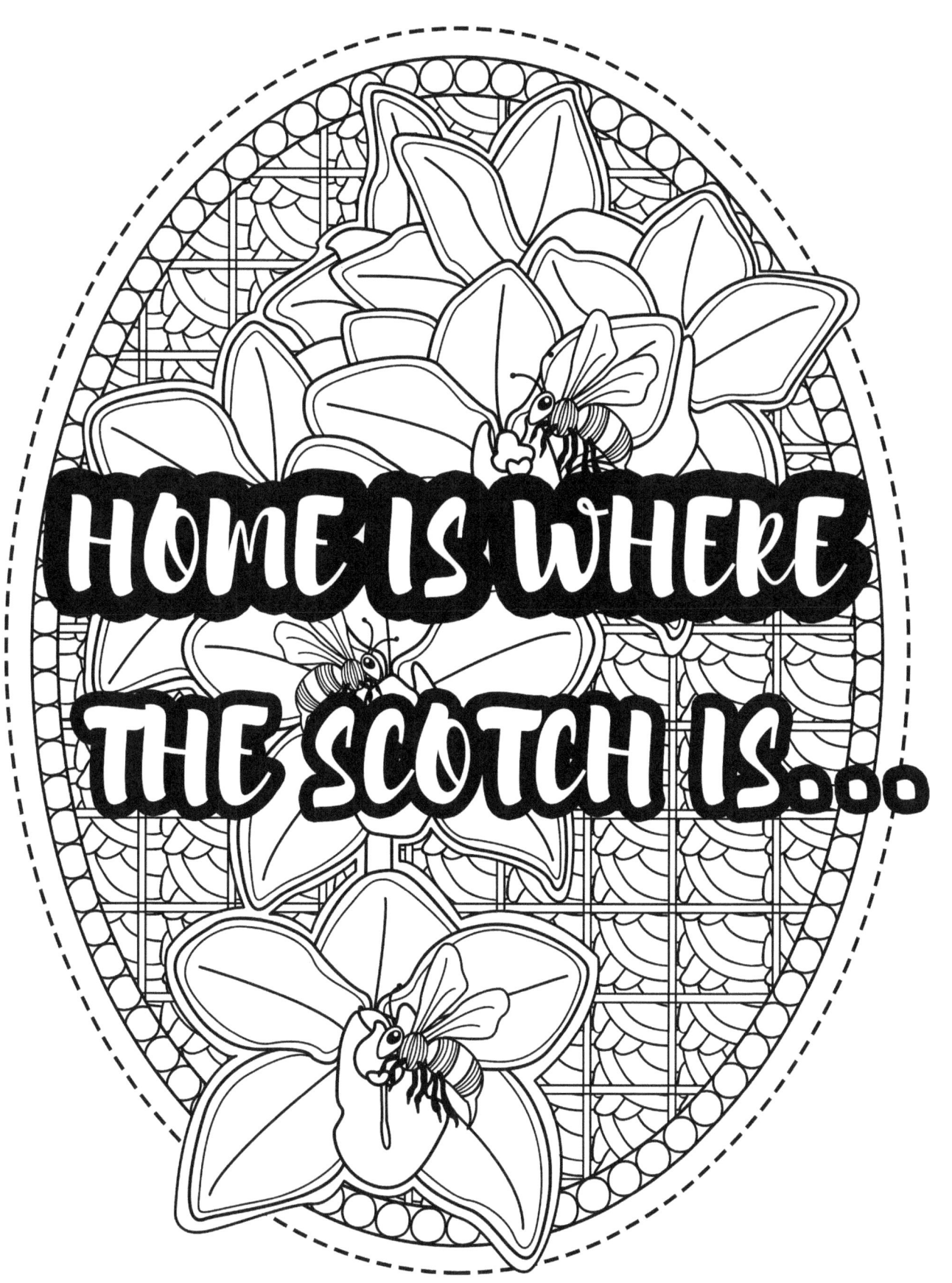

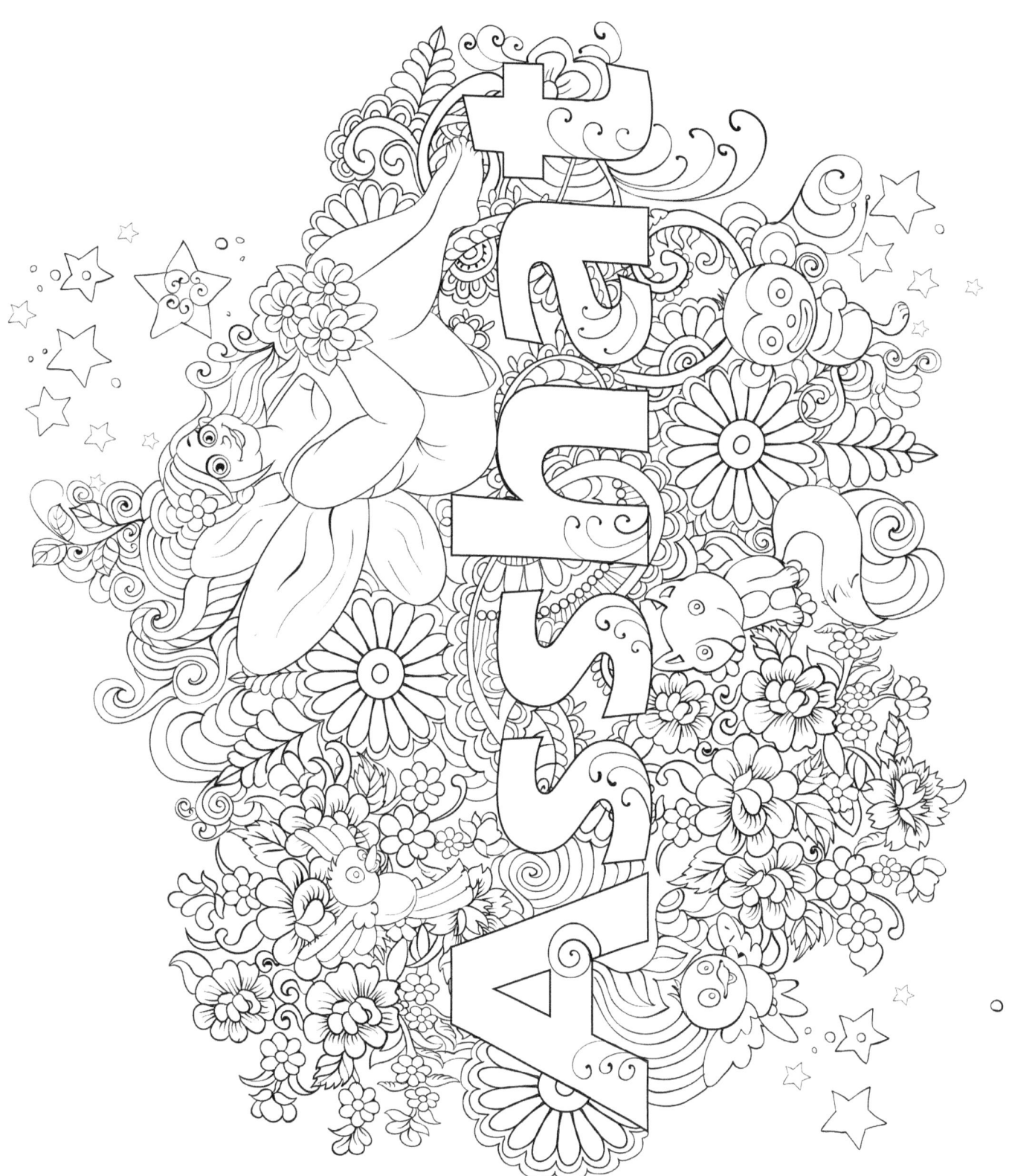

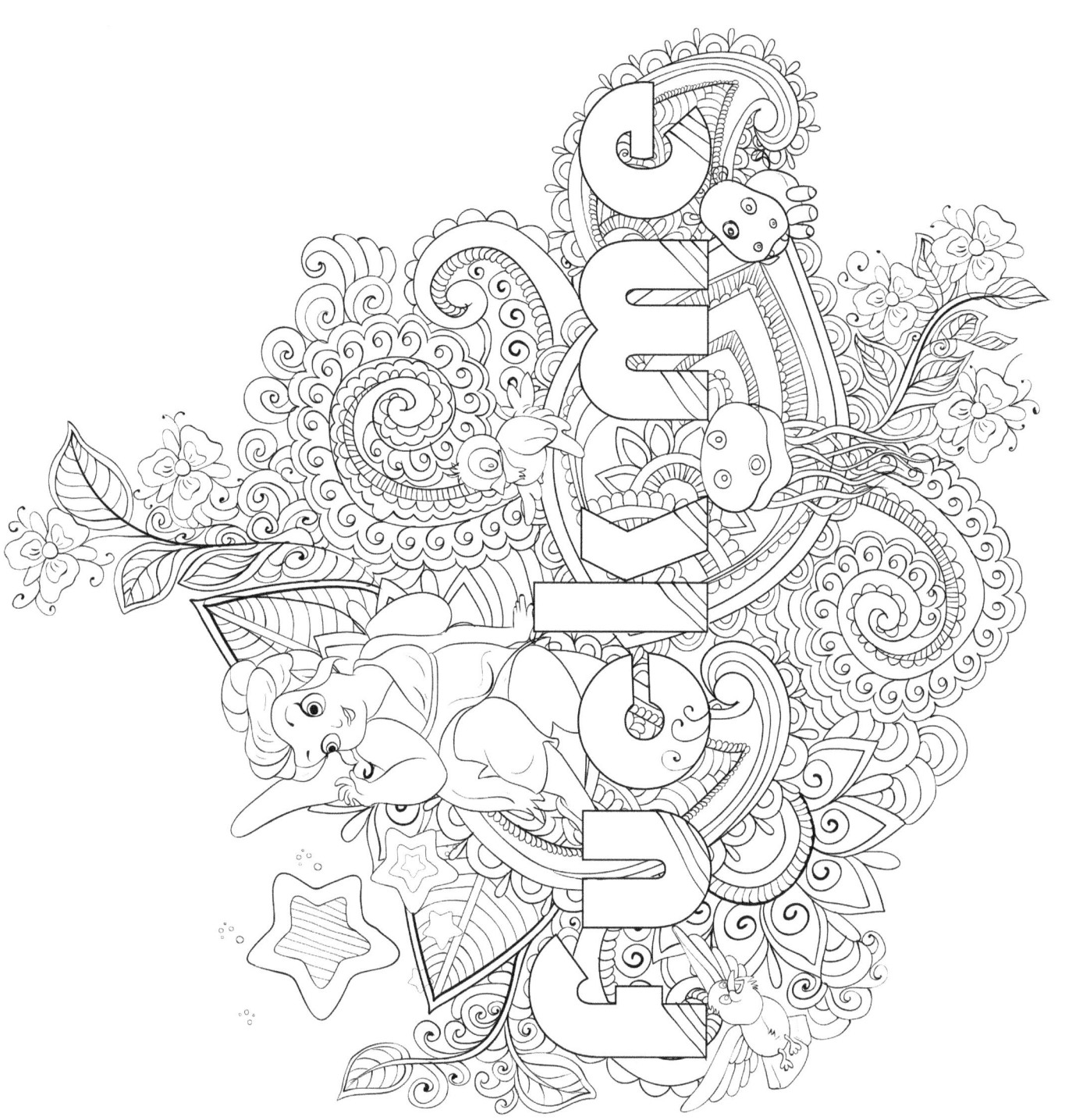

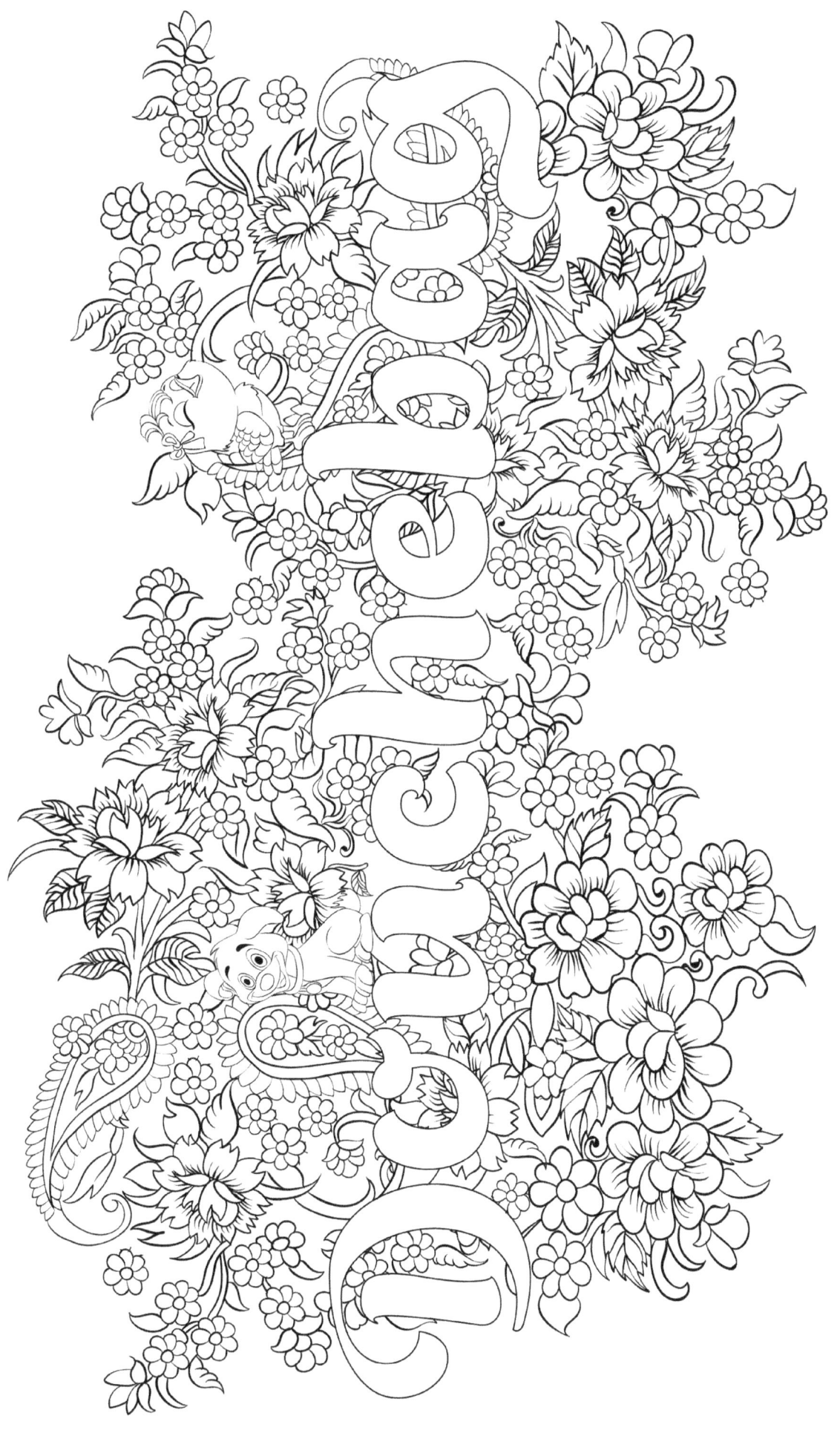

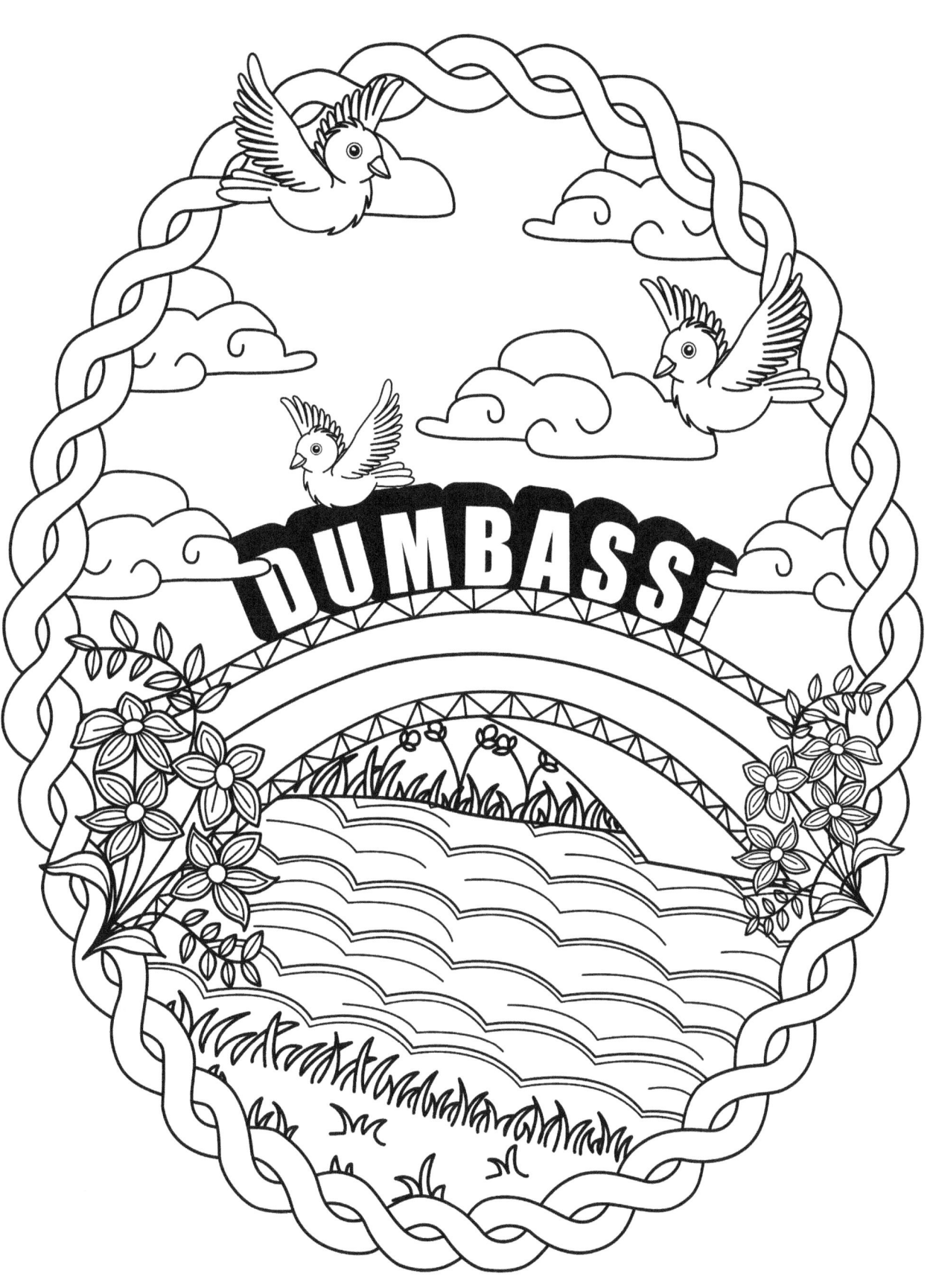

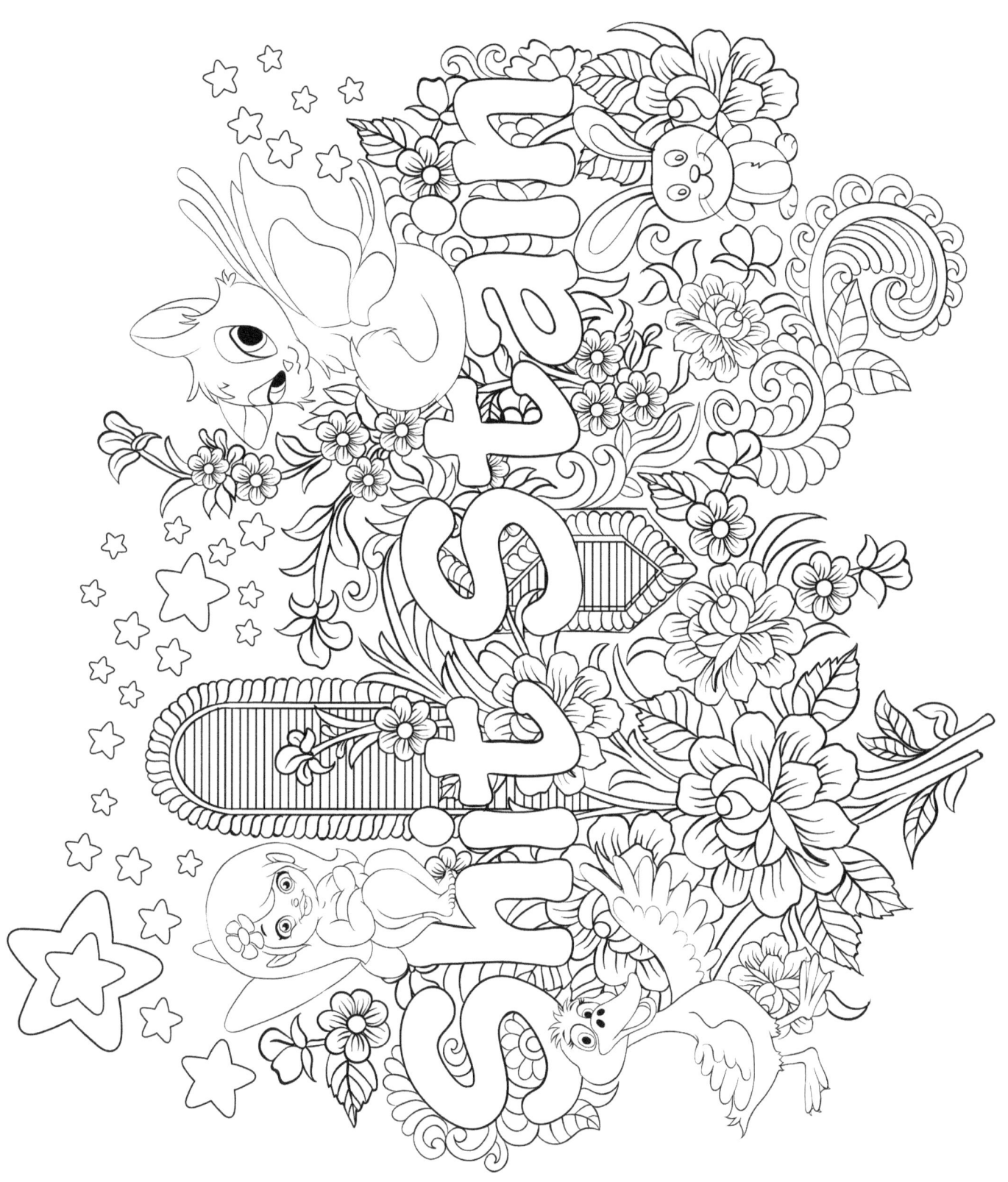

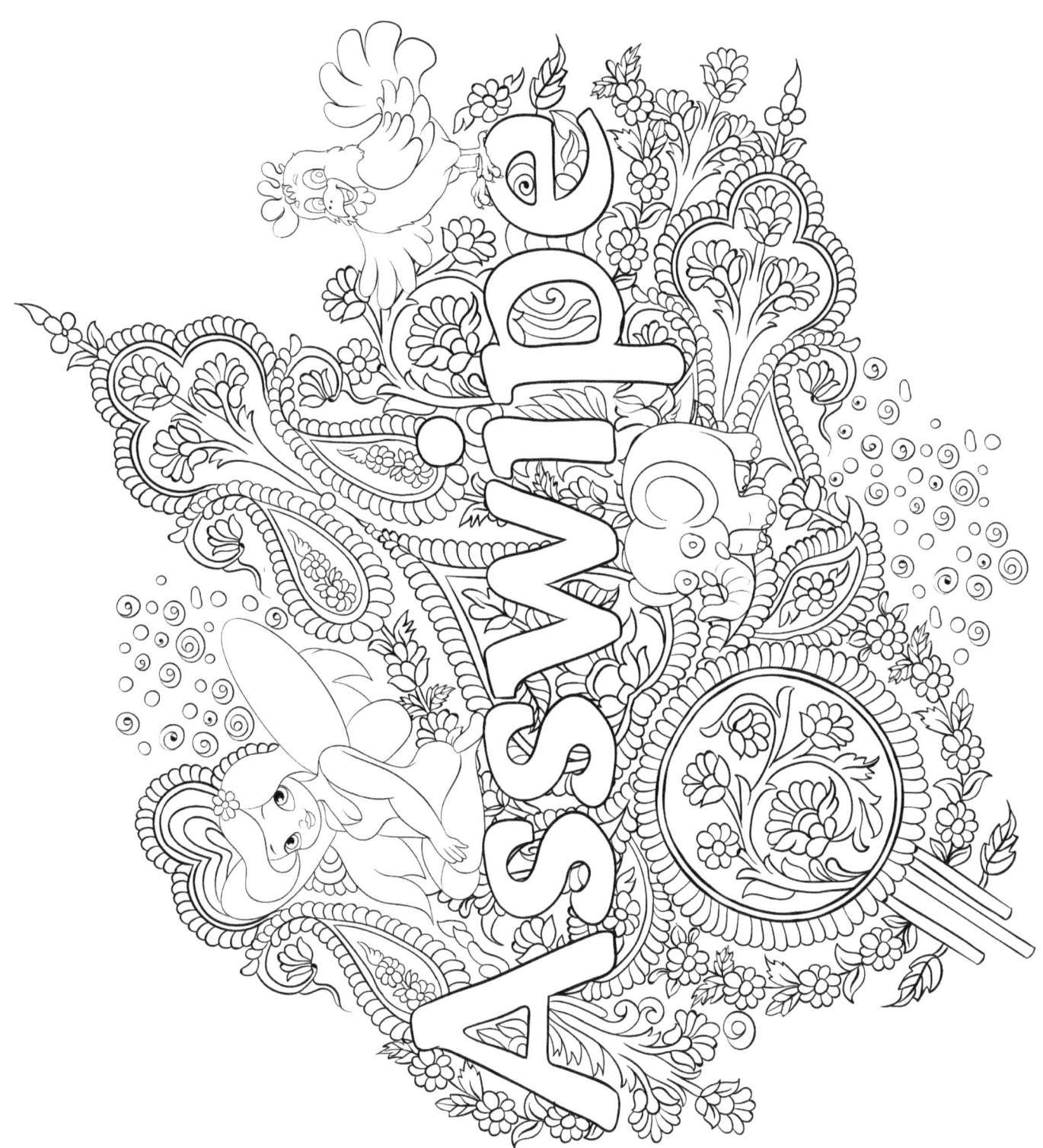

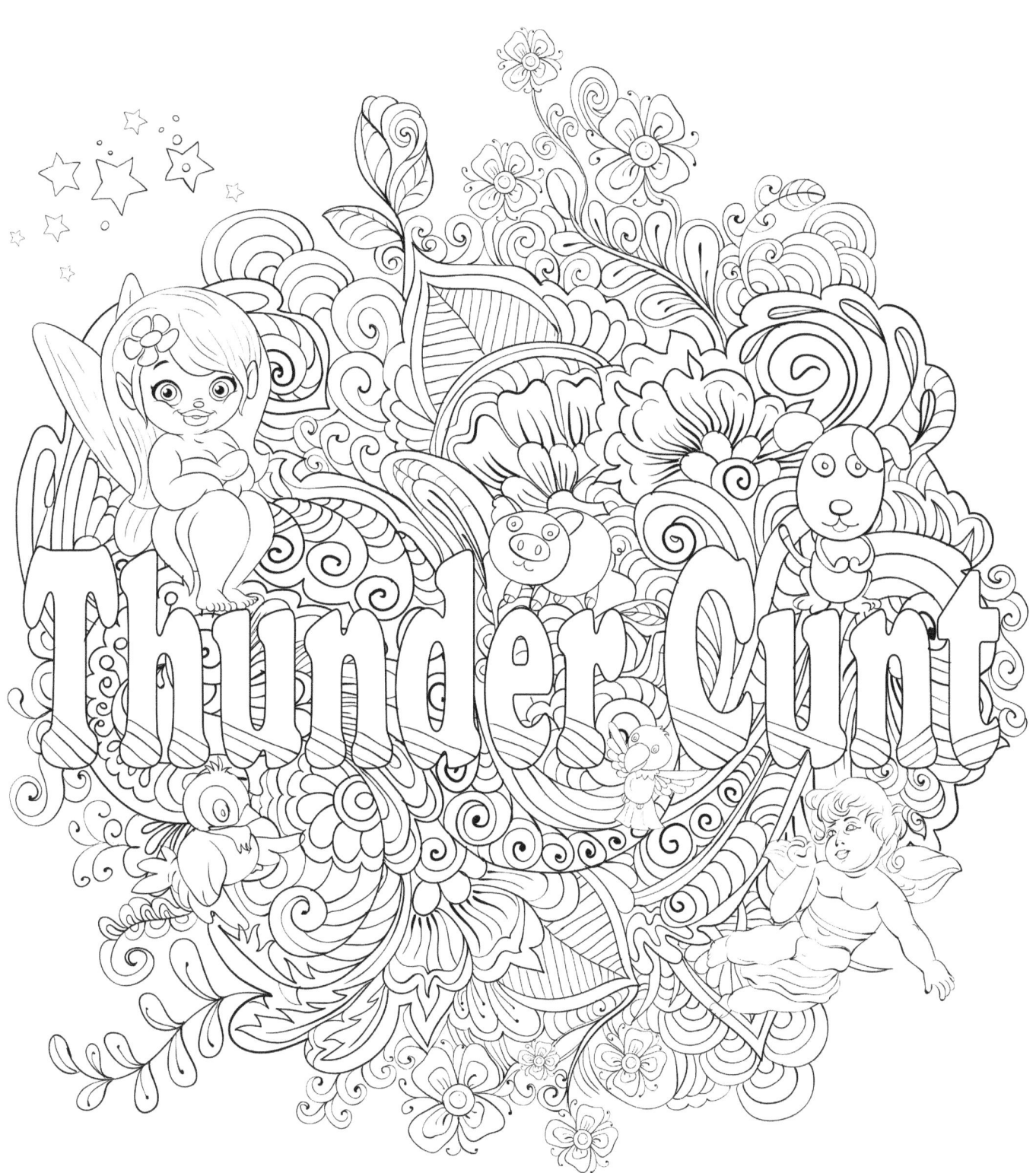

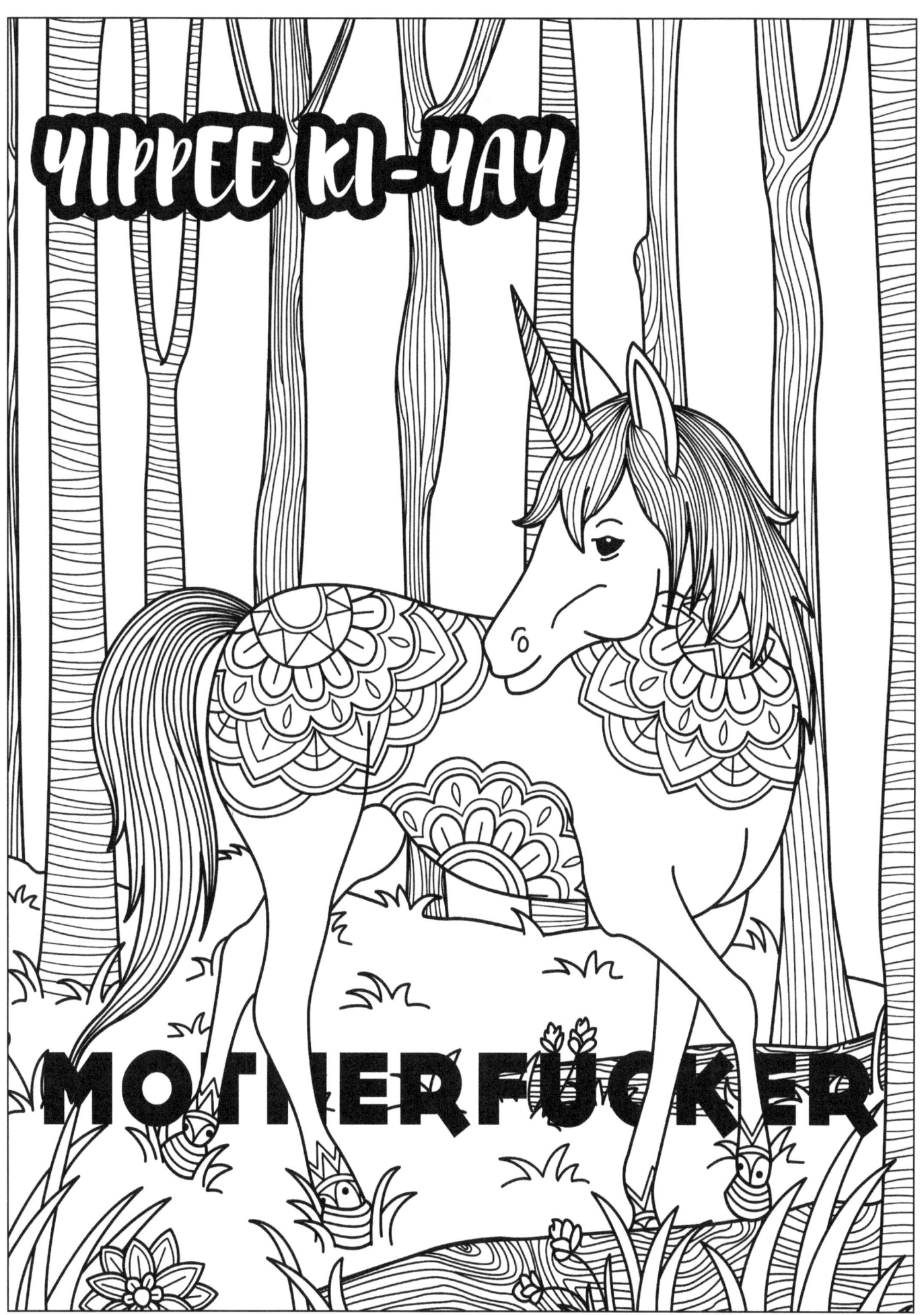

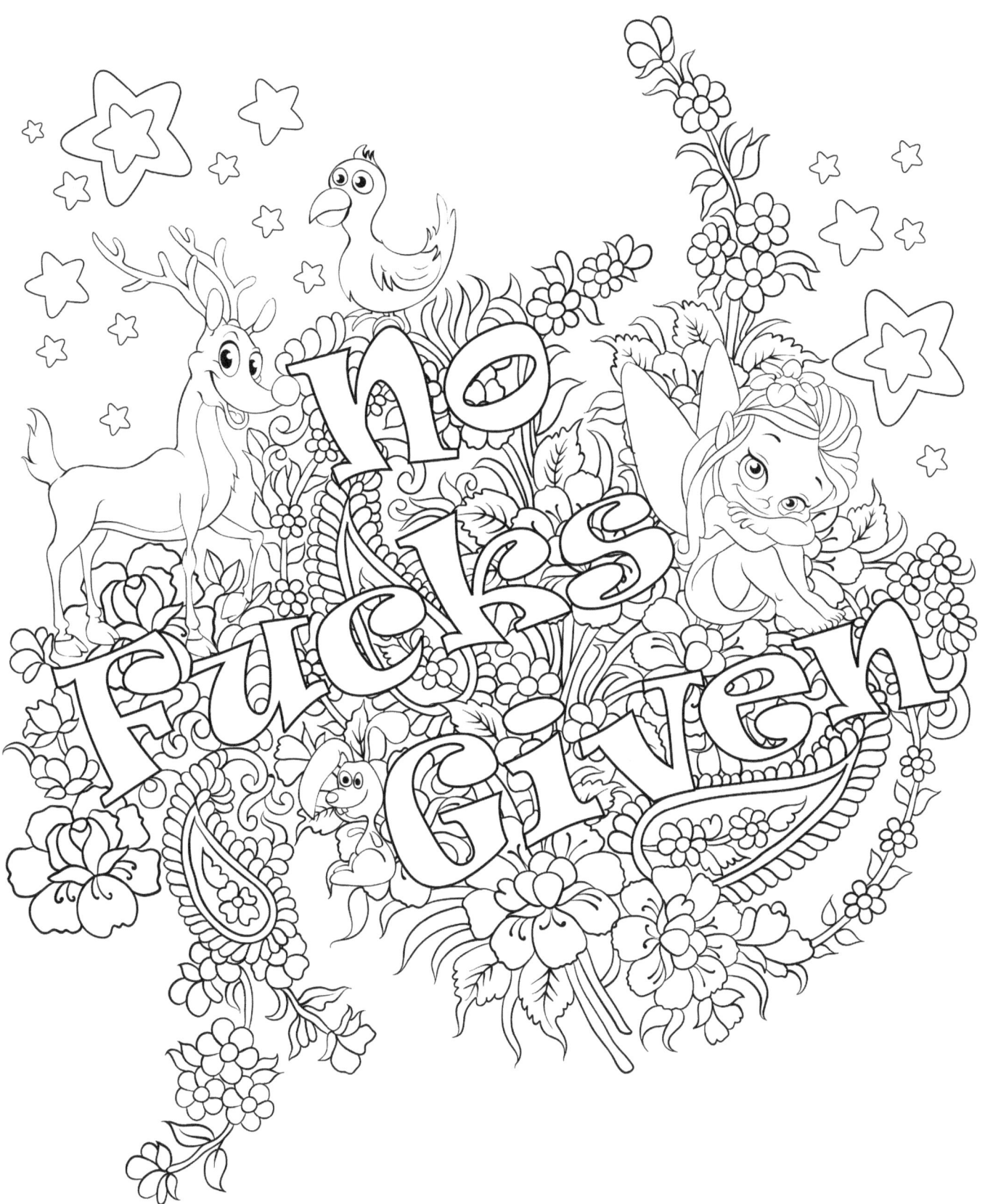

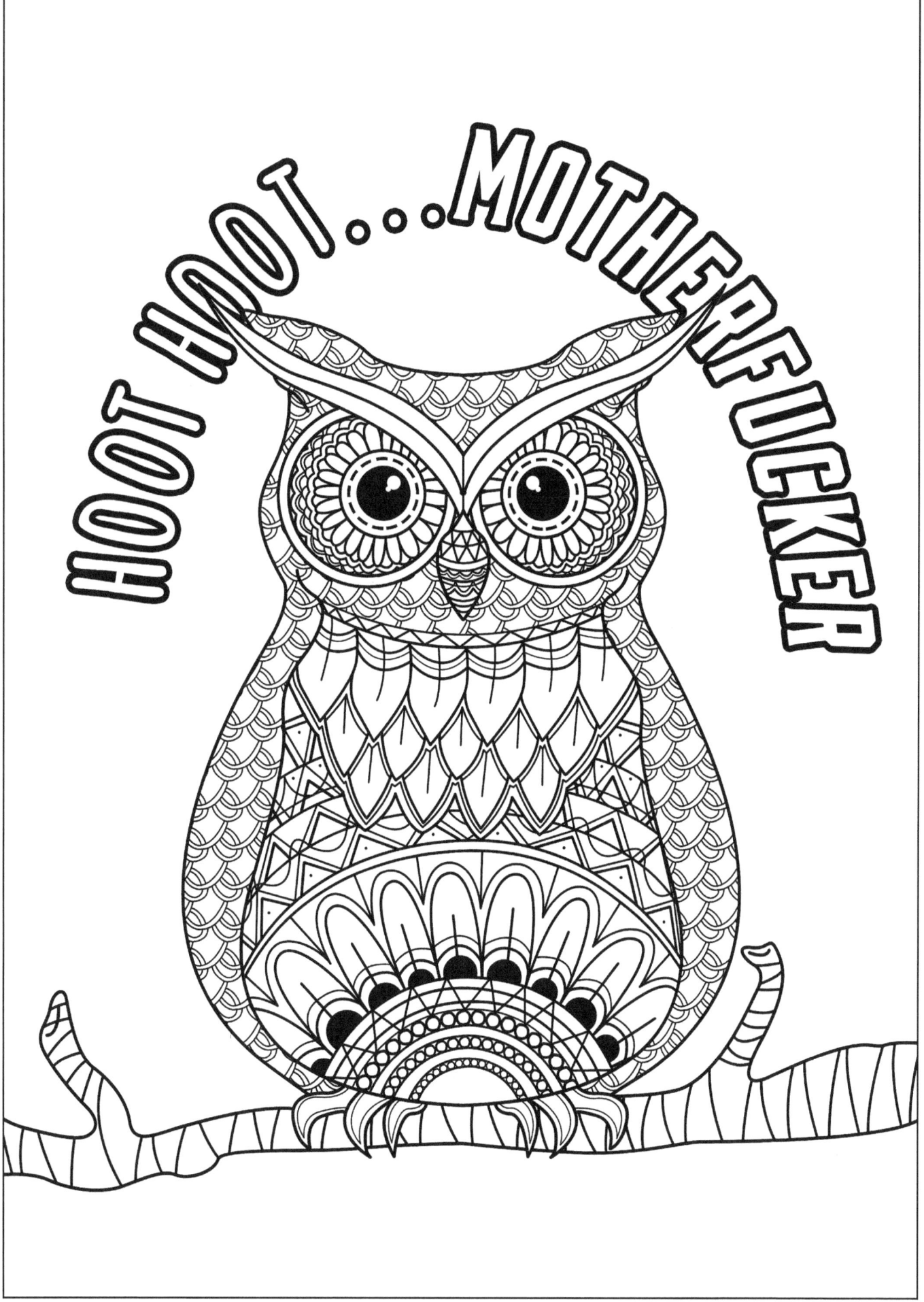

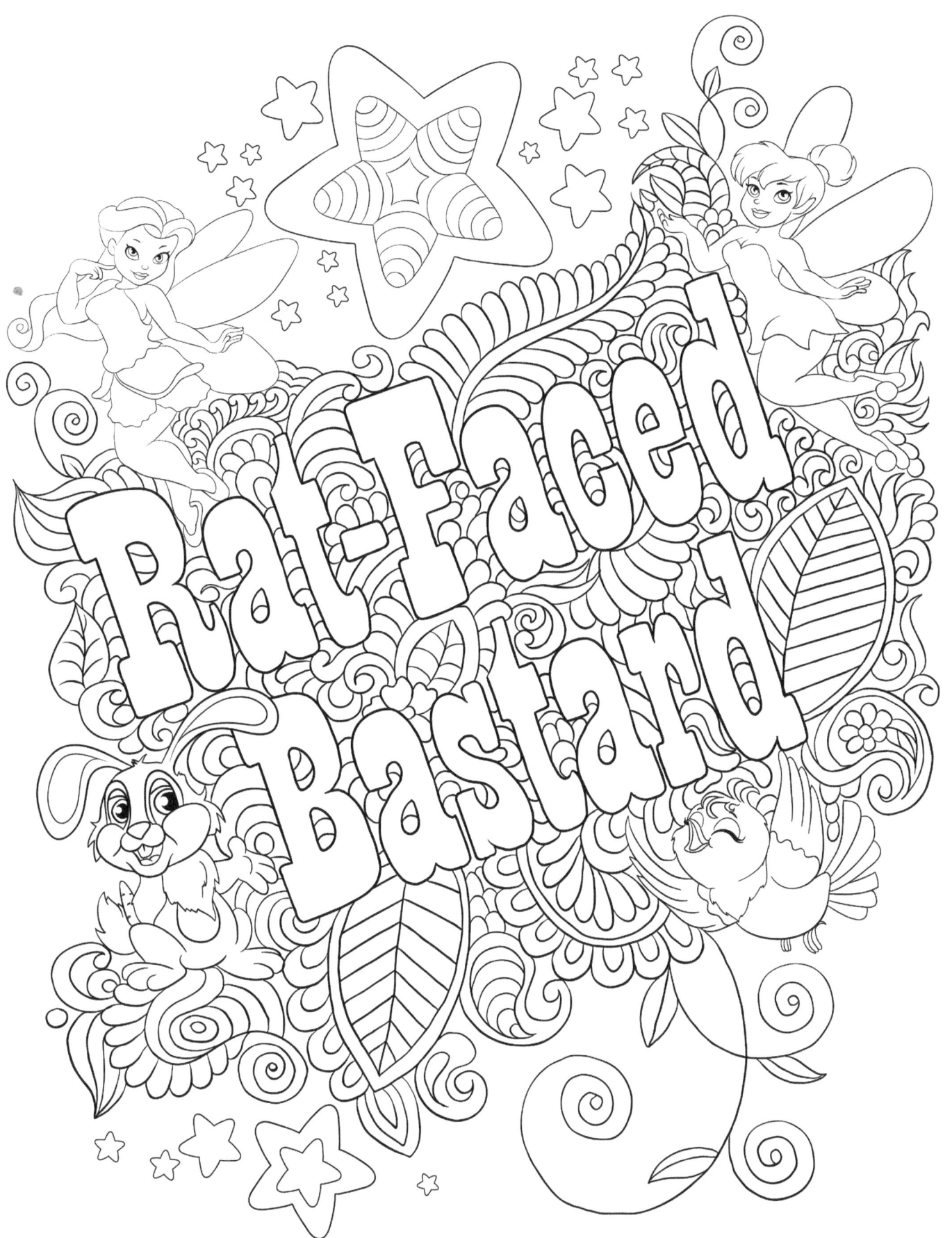

ISBN: 978-1523765737
Copyrights © 2016 All rights reserved
by: Swearing Coloring Book for Adults
Artists:
  Mandala & Caricature Illustration
  Joshua Lazana Lagman and Jade Villaremo

www.ingramcontent.com/pod-product-compliance
Lightning Source LLC
Chambersburg PA
CBHW080636190526

45169CB00009B/3406